Will You Come to Mass?

By Susan Joy Bellavance

Illustrations by Sara Tang

Available from:
Marian Helpers Center
Stockbridge, MA 01263
1-800-462-7426
marian.org
ShopMercy.org

ISBN: 978-1-59614-430-9
Library of Congress Control Number: 2018944187

Imprimi Potest:
Very Rev. Kazimierz Chwalek, MIC
Provincial Superior
The Blessed Virgin Mary, Mother of Mercy Province
May 8, 2018

Nihil Obstat:
Dr. Robert A. Stackpole, STD
Censor Deputatus
May 8, 2018

This book is printed with soy-based ink.

Printed in the United States of America

MARIAN PRESS
STOCKBRIDGE MA 01263

Susan Bellavance served with the Missionaries of Charity, was a Catholic elementary and junior high school teacher, and founding member of Mount Royal Academy in Sunapee, New Hampshire. She also served as a catechist and as a youth group leader. In addition to writing, Susan is a Marian Helper who currently volunteers at Bishop Peterson Residence, a home for retired and elderly priests in the Diocese of Manchester. She resides with her cherished husband, Dale, and two treasured daughters, Sophia and Marguerite, in New Hampshire.

Dedication

To the Eucharistic Heart of Jesus, worthy of all our love.

– SJB

For my goddaughters Guinevere Joan,
Magdalene Rosemary, and Hyacinth Anne.

– SMT

The church bells in the little town ring out like angel voices. "Come, come, come," they sing. "Come to Holy Mass!"

1

The wind carries the angel song everywhere; through the streets and in the lanes, to the homes and the shops, through the hills and the fields.

2

"Come!" they sing.
"Come!" they ring. "Come to Holy Mass!"
But who will come?

"Come!" they sing.
"Come!" they ring.
"Come to Holy Mass!"

"Not me, hee, hee, hee, hee!" says the monkey,
"I've got a game to play!" He runs down the field
while all the people cheer.

And still the bells call.
"Come!" they sing.
"Come!" they ring.
"Come to Holy Mass!"

5

"Oh my," trumpets the elephant in his big comfy slippers on his big comfy chair. "I can never remember what time it starts!"

And still the bells chime.
"Come!" they sing.
"Come!" they ring. "Come to Holy Mass!"

"I'm busy, busy, busy," chirps the robin.
"I have a nest to tidy. My young are coming!"

And still the bells sound.
"Come!" they sing.
"Come!" they ring.
"Come to Holy Mass!"

"No time! No time!" chatters the squirrel.
"I'm gathering and gathering.
You can never have enough!"

And still the bells peal.
"Come!" they sing.
"Come!" they ring. "Come to Holy Mass!"

"Hhhmmm, mmmm," yawns the sleepy sloth.
"I'm...I'm...I'm too tired in the morning, I just want to sleep."
He pulls a pillow on his ear, and over he rolls.

And still the bells invite.
"Come!" they sing.
"Come!" they ring.
"Come to Holy Mass!"

9

"Ssso sssorry," says the snake at the lake.
"I'm sssunning on the sssand."

And still the bells toll.
"Come!" they sing.
"Come!" they ring.
"Come to Holy Mass!"

"It's the weekend!" honk-honk the wild geese.
"We're traveling!"

And still the bells beckon.
"Come!" they sing.
"Come!" they ring.
"Come to Holy Mass!"

"No wheheheh," whinnies the workhorse.
"My fields come first!"

And still the bells knell.
"Come!" they sing.
"Come!" they ring. "Come to Holy Mass!"

"No thanks," the raccoon cheetles.
"It's just not very entertaining."

And still the bells echo.
"Come!" they sing.
"Come!" they ring. "Come to Holy Mass!"

The hyena just laughs at the idea.

And still the bells summon.
"Come!" they sing.
"Come!" they ring. "Come to Holy Mass!"

The little lamb playing out in the fields hears the angel song of the bells. In his heart, he feels a sparkle.

"Yes!" says the little lamb. "I can go to Mass. I want to go. Just lead me there!"

And he follows the
angel song right
up to the door.

Can you find
the little lamb?

18

"I love you, Jesus,"
says the little lamb.
Jesus is consoled. He
holds the little lamb
to His Heart.

"You are mine forever"
Jesus says. "Yes, I am,"
says the little lamb.

Jesus blesses him, and the little lamb smiles.

Now let's play!

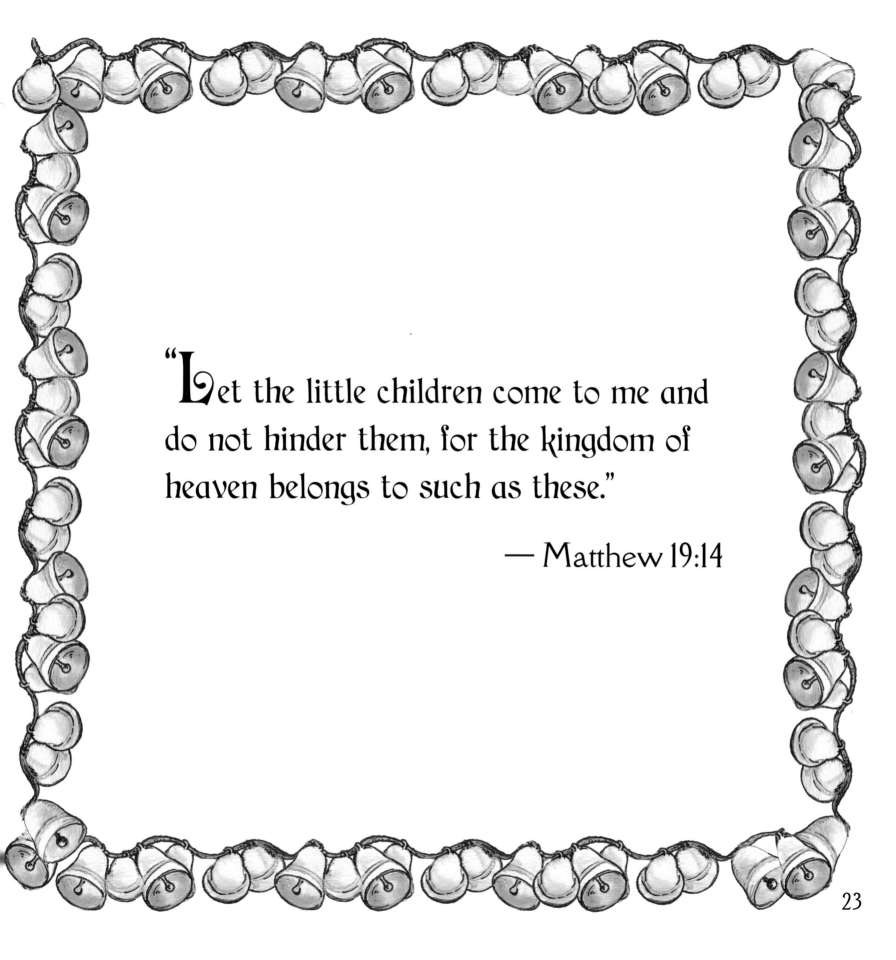

"Let the little children come to me and do not hinder them, for the kingdom of heaven belongs to such as these."

— Matthew 19:14

The End